Department of the Treasury
Office of Inspector General

Small Business Lending Fund Program
Oversight Office
Fiscal Year 2013 Audit Work Plan

Contents

Foreword

This annual work plan outlines the fiscal year 2013 audit priorities for the Office of Small Business Lending Fund (SBLF) Program Oversight within the Treasury Office of Inspector General. The plan provides brief descriptions of new and ongoing audits and reviews that the SBLF Program Oversight Office plans to pursue with respect to the Department's two small business lending programs—the SBLF program and State Small Business Credit Initiative (SSBCI). Although the Work Plan is published annually, continuous adjustments are made to the plan throughout the year as appropriate. The audit priorities for the Office of SBLF Program Oversight are also presented in the Treasury Office of Inspector General Annual Plan for Fiscal Year 2013.

What is our Responsibility?

Our organization was created to protect the integrity of SBLF and SSBCI programs and operations by detecting and preventing fraud, waste, and abuse; identifying opportunities to improve program economy, efficiency, and effectiveness; and holding accountable those who do not meet program requirements or who violate Federal laws.

As required by the Small Business Jobs Act, our office is responsible for reporting no less than two times a year on the oversight provided of the SBLF program, and for conducting and supervising audits of the use of funds made available under SSBCI. Any intentional or reckless misuse of SSBCI funds by participating states that is identified by our office must be recouped by Treasury.

How Do We Plan Our Work?

Work planning is a dynamic process, and adjustments are made throughout the year to meet priorities and to anticipate and respond to emerging issues with available resources. In evaluating work plan proposals, priority consideration is given to consider statutory requirements for audits. We also assess the relative risks in the programs for which we have oversight responsibility to identify the areas that are most in need of attention and accordingly, to set priorities for the sequence and proportion of resources to be allocated.

Audit Title	
	Accuracy of Third Quarter 2012 Dividend Rate Adjustments Under the Small Business Lending Fund Program
Objectives	To determine the accuracy of qualified small business lending volumes for the third quarter of 2012 reported by SBLF participants for dividend rate adjustments.
Importance/Justification	Dividend rates on SBLF funding during the first nine quarters after investment can be adjusted downward based on gains in small business lending. Such gains are identified in supplemental reports filed by lenders that are derived from Call Reports. If a downward adjustment is made, the lower rate will be applied to the dollar amount of SBLF capital only up to the amount by which qualified small business lending has increased.
	Treasury relies on each institution to self-report its gains in qualified small business lending and to calculate the dividend rate that should be applied. Institutions may understate their baseline lending activity or overstate their initial quarter-end lending activity due to unfamiliarity with program rules and the desire to qualify for lower dividend rates.
	Prior OIG audits of participant dividend rates have highlighted a large number of inaccuracies in lending volumes reported by participants. If the inaccuracies are large enough, they can affect the dividend or interest rates applied to an institution. Also regardless of whether the errors impact dividend rates paid by participants, such errors result in Treasury misreporting to Congress the amount of small business lending occurring under the SBLF program needed to measure program performance.
Start Date/Status	Final report issued in January 2013

Audit Title	
	Use of SBLF Funds by Participating Institutions
Objectives	To determine (1) how recipient institutions are using funds awarded under the SBLF program, (2) how current small business lending compares to small business lending prior to entering the program for SBLF recipient institutions, and (3) how current changes in small business lending compare to recipients' projections.
Importance/Justification	Under the Small Business Jobs Act and the terms of the SBLF program, participating institutions are not required to use program funds on small business lending. The lack of restrictions on the use of funds has led to concerns that the capital provided banks will be used to help them expand and increase their profitability and competitiveness without increasing small business lending. Concerns have also been expressed that the Small Business Lending Fund will be used as a "backdoor repayment mechanism" for the Troubled Asset Relief Program (TARP), with little increases in small business lending by banks exiting TARP.
	Treasury is required to provide quarterly reports to Congress describing how participating institutions have used the funds they received under the program. In October 2012, Treasury reported that 89 percent of SBLF participants had increased their small business lending over baseline levels. Specifically, bank participants had increased their small business lending by $6.7 billion (or by 18.6 percent) over their aggregate baseline of $36 billion, and Commercial Development Loan Funds increased their small business lending by $174.8 million (or 22.2 percent) over a $786.7 million baseline. While the report discussed small business lending, it did not identify other uses of SBLF funds. Further, because lending gains reported are cumulative against a June 2010 baseline, it is unclear how much of the gains occurred immediately preceding each institution's entry into the program and what the increases in lending were from that projected in small business lending plans submitted by institutions when applying to the program.
Start Date/Status	October 2012

Audit Title	
	Accuracy of Fourth Quarter 2012 Dividend Rate Adjustments Under the Small Business Lending Fund Program
Objectives	To determine the accuracy of qualified small business lending volumes for the fourth quarter of 2012 reported by SBLF participants for dividend rate adjustments.
Importance/Justification	Dividend rates on SBLF funding during the first nine quarters after investment can be adjusted downward based on gains in small business lending. Such gains are identified in supplemental reports filed by lenders that are derived from Call Reports. If a downward adjustment is made, the lower rate will be applied to the dollar amount of SBLF capital only up to the amount by which qualified small business lending has increased.
	Treasury relies on each institution to self-report its gains in qualified small business lending and to calculate the dividend rate that should be applied. Institutions may understate their baseline lending activity or overstate their initial quarter-end lending activity due to unfamiliarity with program rules and the desire to qualify for lower dividend rates.
	Prior OIG audits of participant dividend rates have highlighted a large number of inaccuracies in lending volumes reported by participants. If the inaccuracies are large enough, they can affect the dividend or interest rates applied to an institution. Also regardless of whether the errors impact dividend rates paid by participants, such errors result in Treasury misreporting to Congress the amount of small business lending occurring under the SBLF program needed to measure program performance.
Start Date/Status	December 2012

Audit Title	
	Review of SBLF Program Office Procedures for Reviewing Participant
Objectives	To determine (1) the effectiveness of SBLF Program review procedures in detecting errors in participant Initial Supplemental Reports (ISR) and Quarterly Supplemental Reports (QSR), (2) whether the review procedures mitigate reporting risk to a tolerable level, and (3) if remediation controls should be developed and incorporated into the review process.
Importance/Justification	Financial institutions participating in the SBLF Program are required to prepare and submit to Treasury initial and supplemental reports of baseline and quarterly small business lending activity. Each report is signed by an executive of the financial institution attesting that the report was prepared in accordance with Treasury's instructions. The information reported establishes (1) the initial lending baseline and dividend rate, (2) the adjusted lending baseline, and (3) the total volume of lending each quarter, which are used to calculate an institution's qualified lending gains and applicable dividend rate. The information is also transmitted to Congress in Treasury's quarterly *Use of Funds Report* to keep Congress informed of program results.
	Appropriate oversight and review of participant reports is essential to ensure that participants comply with SBLF program requirements, Treasury applies the correct dividend rates to investments made under the program, and Congress receives accurate information on small business lending activity attributable to the SBLF funding. Prior SBLF dividend rate audits have identified a high frequency of recording, adjustment, and classification errors in participant reports, causing some dividend rates to be incorrect and Treasury to incorrectly report program activity. The frequency of the errors noted suggests that current oversight procedures performed by the SBLF Program Office are not appropriately designed to mitigate reporting errors.
Start Date/Status	February 2013

Audit Title	
	Accuracy of First Quarter 2013 Dividend Rate Adjustments Under the Small Business Lending Fund Program
Objectives	To determine the accuracy of qualified small business lending volumes for the first quarter of 2013 reported by SBLF participants for dividend rate adjustments.
Importance/Justification	Dividend rates on SBLF funding during the first nine quarters after investment can be adjusted downward based on gains in small business lending. Such gains are identified in supplemental reports filed by lenders that are derived from Call Reports. If a downward adjustment is made, the lower rate will be applied to the dollar amount of SBLF capital only up to the amount by which qualified small business lending has increased.

Treasury relies on each institution to self-report its gains in qualified small business lending and to calculate the dividend rate that should be applied. Institutions may understate their baseline lending activity or overstate their initial quarter-end lending activity due to unfamiliarity with program rules and the desire to qualify for lower dividend rates.

Prior OIG audits of participant dividend rates have highlighted a large number of inaccuracies in lending volumes reported by participants. If the inaccuracies are large enough, they can affect the dividend or interest rates applied to an institution. Also regardless of whether the errors impact dividend rates paid by participants, such errors result in Treasury misreporting to Congress the amount of small business lending occurring under the SBLF program needed to measure program performance. |
| **Start Date/Status** | February 2013 |

Audit Title	
	Factors Influencing the Use of SBLF Funds by Participating Institutions
Objectives	To determine (1) factors that influence how recipient institutions are using funds awarded under the SBLF program, (2) how the SBLF funding contributed to changes in financial data reported by participants, and (3) factors influencing participants' exit from the Troubled Asset Relief Program (TARP).
Importance/Justification	Under the Small Business Jobs Act and the terms of the SBLF program, participating institutions are not required to use program funds on small business lending. The lack of restrictions on the use of funds has led to concerns that the capital provided financial institutions will be used to help them expand and increase their profitability and competitiveness without increasing small business lending. Concerns have also been expressed that the Small Business Lending Fund has been used as a "backdoor repayment mechanism" for TARP, with little increases in small business lending by banks exiting TARP. Treasury's report from its recent Lending Survey of recipients will explain broadly how participants report using their SBLF funds. Through a survey, we will obtain more detailed information on what factors influenced each of the uses of the SBLF funds to gain a better understanding of actions participants have taken related to Treasury's investment. We will also ask participants to explain how the SBLF funding contributed to changes we observed in their financial data. Finally, we will ask former TARP participants admitted to the SBLF program what factors influenced their exit from TARP.
Start Date/Status	February 2013

Audit Title	
	Accuracy of Qualified Small Business Lending Gains for Community Development Loan Funds
Objectives	To determine (1) the accuracy of qualified small business lending volumes reported by Community Development Loan Funds (CDLFs) for the first quarter 2013, (2) whether CDLFs assume greater risk on loan participations with banks through subordinations, (3) the extent to which CDLFs are meeting their quarterly dividend obligations compared to non-CDLF participants in SBLF, and (4) how many CDLFs received both SBLF and SSBCI funding.
Importance/Justification	CDLFs play a critical role in distressed communities that lack access to mainstream financial services by providing facility or operating capital to businesses and providing financing to low-income individuals looking to purchase or rehabilitate their homes. The 52 CDLFs participating in the SBLF program comprise 15 percent of all SBLF participants, and collectively received 3 percent of the $4.1 billion invested under the program. Unlike other participants, CDLFs pay a fixed dividend rate of 2 percent for the first 8 years of participation.

Treasury relies on CDLFs to self-report qualified small business lending gains made with SBLF funds; however, each CDLF may categorize loans in their portfolios incorrectly due unfamiliarity with program rules. Also because CDLFs are unregulated financial institutions, their activity reports are not subject to verification as are other regulated institutions participating in the SBLF program. Although quarterly reporting for the SBLF program does not affect dividend rated for CDLFs in the first 8 years of program participation, inaccuracies in reporting may impact the accuracy of Treasury's reports to Congress on the results of the program. volumes. |
| **Start Date/Status** | May 2013 |

Audit Title	**Treasury's Application of Dividend Rates to SBLF Capital and Oversight of Participant Payments**
Objectives	To determine whether Treasury (1) is correctly applying dividend rates to investment amounts awarded participating institutions, (2) assessing former TARP participants additional fees when quarterly lending has not increased over baseline lending; and (3) effectively managing delinquent and inaccurate payments.
Importance/Justification	Financial institutions participating in the SBLF Program are required to make quarterly interest or dividend payments to Treasury. For non-CDLF institutions, payments are calculated by applying interest rates, which fluctuate based upon an institution's aggregate qualified small business lending gains. Treasury determines the quarterly dividend or interest owed based on small business lending gains reported by respective institutions in the SBLF Program. Any dividend reductions are applied only to the portion of SBLF capital that represents an increase over the baseline lending volume. Additionally, former TARP institutions participating in SBLF are to be assessed added fees if their small business lending has not increased relative to their baseline amount.

Dividends owed under the SBLF program are noncumulative, allowing banks to miss payments or to not pay them at all. However if an institution fails to make dividend payments, Treasury may prohibit it from repurchasing or paying dividends on any securities that are junior to Treasury's securities. Any default that continues for five quarters will provide Treasury the right to appoint an observer on the institution's board of directors.

Limited program resources and the volume of information that must be reviewed quarterly by Treasury may hinder Treasury's ability to effectively oversee the dividend payment process. |
| **Start Date/Status** | May 2013 |

Audit Title	
	Vermont's Use of SSBCI Funds
Objectives	To test participant compliance with program requirements and prohibitions to identify reckless or intentional misuse of SSBCI funds.
Importance/Justification	In May 2011, Treasury awarded the State of Vermont $13.2 million in SSBCI Funds. The state's allocation is disbursed in three tranches, and as of January 2013, Vermont had received the first and second tranches of funding, totaling $4.3 million. Primary oversight of the use of SSBCI funds is the responsibility of each participating state. To ensure that funds are properly controlled and expended, the Act requires that Treasury execute an Allocation Agreement with participants setting forth internal controls, and compliance and reporting requirements. The Act requires the Treasury Office of Inspector General (OIG) to conduct audits of the use of funds made available under SSBCI and to identify any instances of reckless or intentional misuse. The Act also requires Treasury to recoup any funds that the OIG identifies was intentionally or recklessly misused.
Start Date/Status	Report Issued in November 2012

Audit Title	
	Michigan's Use of SSBCI Funds
Objectives	To test participant compliance with program requirements and prohibitions to identify reckless or intentional misuse of SSBCI funds.
Importance/Justification	In July 2011, Treasury awarded the State of Michigan $79.2 million in SSBCI Funds. The state's allocation is disbursed in three tranches, and as of January 2013, Michigan had received the first and second tranches of funding, totaling $52.2 million. Primary oversight of the use of SSBCI funds is the responsibility of each participating state. To ensure that funds are properly controlled and expended, the Act requires that Treasury execute an Allocation Agreement with participants setting forth internal controls, and compliance and reporting requirements. The Act requires the Treasury Office of Inspector General (OIG) to conduct audits of the use of funds made available under SSBCI and to identify any instances of reckless or intentional misuse. The Act also requires Treasury to recoup any funds that the OIG identifies was intentionally or recklessly misused.
Start Date/Status	Report Issued in December 2012

Audit Title	Texas' Use of SSBCI Funds
Objectives	To test participant compliance with program requirements and prohibitions to identify reckless or intentional misuse of SSBCI funds.
Importance/Justification	In August 2011, Treasury awarded the State of Texas $46.6 million in SSBCI funds. The state's allocation is disbursed in three tranches, and as of January 2013, Texas had received the first tranche of funding, totaling $15.4 million. These funds were distributed to the state's Venture Capital Program. The state is eligible for additional disbursements once it certifies that it has obligated, transferred or spent at least 80 percent of its first tranche of funds. Primary oversight of the use of SSBCI funds is the responsibility of each participating state. To ensure that funds are properly controlled and expended, the Act requires that Treasury execute an Allocation Agreement with participants setting forth internal controls, and compliance and reporting requirements. The Act requires the Treasury Office of Inspector General (OIG) to conduct audits of the use of funds made available under SSBCI and to identify any instances of reckless or intentional misuse. The Act also requires Treasury to recoup any funds that the OIG identifies was intentionally or recklessly misused.
Start Date/Status	Report issued in January 2013

Audit Title	
	Missouri's Use of SSBCI Funds
Objectives	To test participant compliance with program requirements and prohibitions to identify reckless or intentional misuse of SSBCI funds.
Importance/Justification	In May 2011, Treasury awarded the state of Missouri $26.9 million in SSBCI funds. The state's allocation is disbursed in three tranches, and as of January 2013, Missouri had received the first and second tranches, totaling $17.8 million. The funds were distributed to the state's two small business programs—a Loan Participation Program and a Venture Capital Program. The state is eligible for additional disbursements once it certifies that it has obligated, transferred or spent at least 80 percent of its second tranche of funds. Primary oversight of the use of SSBCI funds is the responsibility of each participating state. To ensure that funds are properly controlled and expended, the Act requires that Treasury execute an Allocation Agreement with participants setting forth internal controls, and compliance and reporting requirements. The Act requires the Treasury Office of Inspector General (OIG) to conduct audits of the use of funds made available under SSBCI and to identify any instances of reckless or intentional misuse. The Act also requires Treasury to recoup any funds that the OIG identifies was intentionally or recklessly misused.
Start Date/Status	August 2012

Audit Title	
	Massachusetts' Use of SSBCI Funds
Objectives	To test participant compliance with program requirements and prohibitions to identify reckless or intentional misuse of SSBCI funds.
Importance/Justification	In September 2011, Treasury awarded the state of Massachusetts $22 million in SSBCI funds. The state's allocation is disbursed in three tranches, and as of January 2013, Massachusetts had received the first tranche of funding, totaling $7.3 million. These funds were distributed to the state's three small business lending programs – a Capital Access Program and two Loan Participation Programs. The state is eligible for additional disbursements once it certifies that it has obligated, transferred or spent at least 80 percent of its first tranche of funds.
	Primary oversight of the use of SSBCI funds is the responsibility of each participating state. To ensure that funds are properly controlled and expended, the Act requires that Treasury execute an Allocation Agreement with participants setting forth internal controls, and compliance and reporting requirements.
	The Act requires the Treasury Office of Inspector General (OIG) to conduct audits of the use of funds made available under SSBCI and to identify any instances of reckless or intentional misuse. The Act also requires Treasury to recoup any funds that the OIG identifies was intentionally or recklessly misused.
Start Date/Status	August 2012

Audit Title	
	Kansas' Use of SSBCI Funds
Objectives	To test participant compliance with program requirements and prohibitions to identify reckless or intentional misuse of SSBCI funds.
Importance/Justification	In June 2011, Treasury awarded the state of Kansas $13.2 million in SSBCI funds. The state's allocation is disbursed in three tranches, and as of January 2013, Kansas had received the first and second tranches of funding, totaling $8.7 million. These funds were distributed to the state's two small business lending programs—a Loan Participation Program and a Venture Capital Program. The state is eligible for additional disbursements once it certifies that it has obligated, transferred or spent at least 80 percent of its second tranche of funds.

Primary oversight of the use of SSBCI funds is the responsibility of each participating state. To ensure that funds are properly controlled and expended, the Act requires that Treasury execute an Allocation Agreement with participants setting forth internal controls, and compliance and reporting requirements.

The Act requires the Treasury Office of Inspector General (OIG) to conduct audits of the use of funds made available under SSBCI and to identify any instances of reckless or intentional misuse. The Act also requires Treasury to recoup any funds that the OIG identifies was intentionally or recklessly misused. |
| **Start Date/Status** | September 2012 |

Audit Title	
	New Jersey's Use of SSBCI Funds
Objectives	To test participant compliance with program requirements and prohibitions to identify reckless or intentional misuse of SSBCI funds.
Importance/Justification	In September 2011, Treasury awarded the state of New Jersey $33.8 million in SSBCI funds. The state's allocation is disbursed in three tranches, and as of January 2013, New Jersey had received the first tranche of funding, totaling $11.1 million. These funds were distributed to the state's four small business lending programs—a Direct Lending Program, Loan Guarantee Program, Loan Participation Program and a Venture Capital Program. The state is eligible for additional disbursements once it certifies that it has obligated, transferred or spent at least 80 percent of its first tranche of funds. Primary oversight of the use of SSBCI funds is the responsibility of each participating state. To ensure that funds are properly controlled and expended, the Act requires that Treasury execute an Allocation Agreement with participants setting forth internal controls, and compliance and reporting requirements. The Act requires the Treasury Office of Inspector General (OIG) to conduct audits of the use of funds made available under SSBCI and to identify any instances of reckless or intentional misuse. The Act also requires Treasury to recoup any funds that the OIG identifies was intentionally or recklessly misused.
Start Date/Status	November 2012

Audit Title	
	Delaware's Use of SSBCI Funds
Objectives	To test participant compliance with program requirements and prohibitions to identify reckless or intentional misuse of SSBCI funds.
Importance/Justification	In July 2011, Treasury awarded the state of Delaware $13.2 million in SSBCI funds. The state's allocation is disbursed in three tranches, and as of January 2013, Delaware had received its first tranche of funding, totaling $4.3 million. These funds were distributed to the state's two small business lending programs – a Capital Access Program and a Loan Participation Program. The state is eligible for additional disbursements once it certifies that it has obligated, transferred or spent at least 80 percent of its first tranche of funds.
	Primary oversight of the use of SSBCI funds is the responsibility of each participating state. To ensure that funds are properly controlled and expended, the Act requires that Treasury execute an Allocation Agreement with participants setting forth internal controls, and compliance and reporting requirements.
	The Act requires the Treasury Office of Inspector General (OIG) to conduct audits of the use of funds made available under SSBCI and to identify any instances of reckless or intentional misuse. The Act also requires Treasury to recoup any funds that the OIG identifies was intentionally or recklessly misused.
Start Date/Status	October 2012

Audit Title	
	Washington's Use of SSBCI Funds
Objectives	To test participant compliance with program requirements and prohibitions to identify reckless or intentional misuse of SSBCI funds.
Importance/Justification	In October 2011, Treasury awarded the state of Washington $19.7 million in SSBCI funds. The state's allocation is disbursed in three tranches, and as of January 2013, Washington had received the first and second tranches of funding, totaling $13 million. These funds were distributed to the state's three small business lending programs –a Loan Participation Program, a Capital Access Program and a Venture Capital Program. The state is eligible for additional disbursements once it certifies that it has obligated, transferred or spent at least 80 percent of its second tranche of funds. Primary oversight of the use of SSBCI funds is the responsibility of each participating state. To ensure that funds are properly controlled and expended, the Act requires that Treasury execute an Allocation Agreement with participants setting forth internal controls, and compliance and reporting requirements. The Act requires the Treasury Office of Inspector General (OIG) to conduct audits of the use of funds made available under SSBCI and to identify any instances of reckless or intentional misuse. The Act also requires Treasury to recoup any funds that the OIG identifies was intentionally or recklessly misused.
Start Date/Status	December 2012

Audit Title	
	Alabama's Use of SSBCI Funds
Objectives	To test participant compliance with program requirements and prohibitions to identify reckless or intentional misuse of SSBCI funds.
Importance/Justification	In August 2011, Treasury awarded the state of Alabama $31.3 million in SSBCI funds. The state's allocation is disbursed in three tranches, and as of January 2013, Alabama had received its first tranche of funding, totaling $10.3 million. These funds were distributed to the state's three small business lending programs –a Capital Access Program, a Loan Participation program and a Loan Guarantee Program. The state is eligible for additional disbursements once it certifies that it has obligated, transferred or spent at least 80 percent of its first tranche of funds. Primary oversight of the use of SSBCI funds is the responsibility of each participating state. To ensure that funds are properly controlled and expended, the Act requires that Treasury execute an Allocation Agreement with participants setting forth internal controls, and compliance and reporting requirements. The Act requires the Treasury Office of Inspector General (OIG) to conduct audits of the use of funds made available under SSBCI and to identify any instances of reckless or intentional misuse. The Act also requires Treasury to recoup any funds that the OIG identifies was intentionally or recklessly misused.
Start Date/Status	December 2012

Audit Title	
	Florida's Use of SSBCI Funds
Objectives	To test participant compliance with program requirements and prohibitions to identify reckless or intentional misuse of SSBCI funds.
Importance/Justification	In August 2011, Treasury awarded the State of Florida $97.7 million in SSBCI funds. The state's allocation is disbursed in three tranches, and as of January 2013, Florida had received the first tranche of funding, totaling $32.2 million. These funds were distributed to the state's seven small business lending programs— two Direct Lending programs, two Loan Guarantee Programs, a Capital Access Program, a Loan Participation Program and a Venture Capital Program. The state is eligible for additional disbursements once it certifies that it has obligated, transferred or spent at least 80 percent of its first tranche of funds.

Primary oversight of the use of SSBCI funds is the responsibility of each participating state. To ensure that funds are properly controlled and expended, the Act requires that Treasury execute an Allocation Agreement with participants setting forth internal controls, and compliance and reporting requirements.

The Act requires the Treasury Office of Inspector General (OIG) to conduct audits of the use of funds made available under SSBCI and to identify any instances of reckless or intentional misuse. The Act also requires Treasury to recoup any funds that the OIG identifies was intentionally or recklessly misused. |
| **Start Date/Status** | January 2013 |

Audit Title	
	Effectiveness of the State Small Business Credit Initiative
Objectives	To (1) assess the effectiveness of SSBCI in increasing access to capital for small businesses, and (2) evaluate the adequacy of Treasury's oversight and management of the program.
Importance/Justification	SSBCI was established to support existing and new state programs that support private financing to small businesses and small manufacturers that are not obtaining the loans or investments they need to expand and create jobs. States are required under the Small Business Jobs Act to report quarterly and annually on their use of SSBCI funds. They are also required to submit to Treasury no later than March 31 of each year an Annual Report providing transaction-level data for each loan or investment made with SSBCI funds. According to Treasury, primary oversight of the use of SSBCI funds is the responsibility of each participating state. In May 2012—nearly a year after most states received their first funding allocation—Treasury issued the *SSBCI National Standards for Compliance and Oversight*, providing states with "best practice" guidance for managing compliance with program requirements. States were not required to adopt the guidance. Although to-date Treasury has not verified state compliance with program requirements, Treasury plans to verify the accuracy of a sample of SSBCI Annual Report data submitted by states based on a comparison of the data to actual loan or investment documentation. While this review will test for compliance with several requirements, such as annual revenue limits of borrowers and the ratio of private credit to SSBCI financing, it will not test for compliance with most program requirements and prohibitions.
Start Date/Status	January 2013

Audit Title	
	North Carolina's Use of SSBCI Funds
Objectives	To test participant compliance with program requirements and prohibitions to identify reckless or intentional misuse of SSBCI funds.
Importance/Justification	In May 2011, Treasury awarded the state of North Carolina $46.1 million in SSBCI funds. The state's allocation is disbursed in three tranches, and as of January 2013, North Carolina had received the first and second tranches of funding, totaling $30.4 million. These funds were distributed to the state's three small business lending programs—a Capital Access Program, a Loan Participation Program and a Venture Capital Program. The state is eligible for additional disbursements once it certifies that it has obligated, transferred or spent at least 80 percent of its second tranche of funds. Primary oversight of the use of SSBCI funds is the responsibility of each participating state. To ensure that funds are properly controlled and expended, the Act requires that Treasury execute an Allocation Agreement with participants setting forth internal controls, and compliance and reporting requirements. The Act requires the Treasury Office of Inspector General (OIG) to conduct audits of the use of funds made available under SSBCI and to identify any instances of reckless or intentional misuse. The Act also requires Treasury to recoup any funds that the OIG identifies was intentionally or recklessly misused.
Start Date/Status	February 2013

Audit Title	
	Illinois' Use of SSBCI Funds
Objectives	To test participant compliance with program requirements and prohibitions to identify reckless or intentional misuse of SSBCI funds.
Importance/Justification	In July 2011, Treasury awarded the state of Illinois $78.4 million in SSBCI funds. The state's allocation is disbursed in three tranches, and as of January 2013, Illinois had received the first tranche of funding, totaling $25.9 million. These funds were distributed to the state's five small business lending programs—a Capital Access Program, a Collateral Support Program, a Direct Lending Program, a Loan Participation Program and a Venture Capital Program. The state is eligible for additional disbursements once it certifies that it has obligated, transferred or spent at least 80 percent of its first tranche of funds. Primary oversight of the use of SSBCI funds is the responsibility of each participating state. To ensure that funds are properly controlled and expended, the Act requires that Treasury execute an Allocation Agreement with participants setting forth internal controls, and compliance and reporting requirements. The Act requires the Treasury Office of Inspector General (OIG) to conduct audits of the use of funds made available under SSBCI and to identify any instances of reckless or intentional misuse. The Act also requires Treasury to recoup any funds that the OIG identifies was intentionally or recklessly misused.
Start Date/Status	April 2013

Audit Title	
	Tennessee's Use of SSBCI Funds
Objectives	To test participant compliance with program requirements and prohibitions to identify reckless or intentional misuse of SSBCI funds.
Importance/Justification	In October 2011, Treasury awarded the state of Tennessee $29.7 million in SSBCI funds. The state's allocation is disbursed in three tranches, and as of January 2013, Tennessee had received the first tranche of funding, totaling $9.8 million. These funds were distributed to the state's small business lending program—a Venture Capital Program. The state is eligible for additional disbursements once it certifies that it has obligated, transferred or spent at least 80 percent of its first tranche of funds.
	Primary oversight of the use of SSBCI funds is the responsibility of each participating state. To ensure that funds are properly controlled and expended, the Act requires that Treasury execute an Allocation Agreement with participants setting forth internal controls, and compliance and reporting requirements.
	The Act requires the Treasury Office of Inspector General (OIG) to conduct audits of the use of funds made available under SSBCI and to identify any instances of reckless or intentional misuse. The Act also requires Treasury to recoup any funds that the OIG identifies was intentionally or recklessly misused.
Start Date/Status	April 2013

Audit Title	New Hampshire's Use of SSBCI Funds
Objectives	To test participant compliance with program requirements and prohibitions to identify reckless or intentional misuse of SSBCI funds.
Importance/Justification	In July 2011, Treasury awarded the state of New Hampshire $13.2 million in SSBCI funds. The state's allocation is disbursed in three tranches, and as of January 2013, New Hampshire had received the first tranche of funding, totaling $4.3 million. These funds were distributed to the state's five small business lending programs—a Loan Participation Program, a Capital Access Program, a Collateral Support Program, a Loan Guarantee Program and a Venture Capital Program. The state is eligible for additional disbursements once it certifies that it has obligated, transferred or spent at least 80 percent of its first tranche of funds.

Primary oversight of the use of SSBCI funds is the responsibility of each participating state. To ensure that funds are properly controlled and expended, the Act requires that Treasury execute an Allocation Agreement with participants setting forth internal controls, and compliance and reporting requirements.

The Act requires the Treasury Office of Inspector General (OIG) to conduct audits of the use of funds made available under SSBCI and to identify any instances of reckless or intentional misuse. The Act also requires Treasury to recoup any funds that the OIG identifies was intentionally or recklessly misused. |
| **Start Date/Status** | May 2013 |

Audit Title	
	South Carolina's Use of SSBCI Funds
Objectives	To test participant compliance with program requirements and prohibitions to identify reckless or intentional misuse of SSBCI funds.
Importance/Justification	In July 2011, Treasury awarded the state of South Carolina $18 million in SSBCI funds. The state's allocation is disbursed in three tranches, and as of January 2013, South Carolina had received the first tranche of funding, totaling $6 million. These funds were distributed to the state's two small business lending programs—a Capital Access Program and a Loan Participation Program. The state is eligible for additional disbursements once it certifies that it has obligated, transferred or spent at least 80 percent of its first tranche of funds. Primary oversight of the use of SSBCI funds is the responsibility of each participating state. To ensure that funds are properly controlled and expended, the Act requires that Treasury execute an Allocation Agreement with participants setting forth internal controls, and compliance and reporting requirements. The Act requires the Treasury Office of Inspector General (OIG) to conduct audits of the use of funds made available under SSBCI and to identify any instances of reckless or intentional misuse. The Act also requires Treasury to recoup any funds that the OIG identifies was intentionally or recklessly misused.
Start Date/Status	June 2013

Audit Title	
	Idaho's Use of SSBCI Funds
Objectives	To test participant compliance with program requirements and prohibitions to identify reckless or intentional misuse of SSBCI funds.
Importance/Justification	In August 2011, Treasury awarded the state of Idaho $13.2 million in SSBCI funds. The state's allocation is disbursed in three tranches, and as of January 2013, Idaho had received the first and second tranches of funding, totaling $8.6 million. These funds were distributed to the state small business lending program—a Collateral Support Program. The state is eligible for additional disbursements once it certifies that it has obligated, transferred or spent at least 80 percent of its second tranche of funds.
	Primary oversight of the use of SSBCI funds is the responsibility of each participating state. To ensure that funds are properly controlled and expended, the Act requires that Treasury execute an Allocation Agreement with participants setting forth internal controls, and compliance and reporting requirements.
	The Act requires the Treasury Office of Inspector General (OIG) to conduct audits of the use of funds made available under SSBCI and to identify any instances of reckless or intentional misuse. The Act also requires Treasury to recoup any funds that the OIG identifies was intentionally or recklessly misused.
Start Date/Status	July 2013